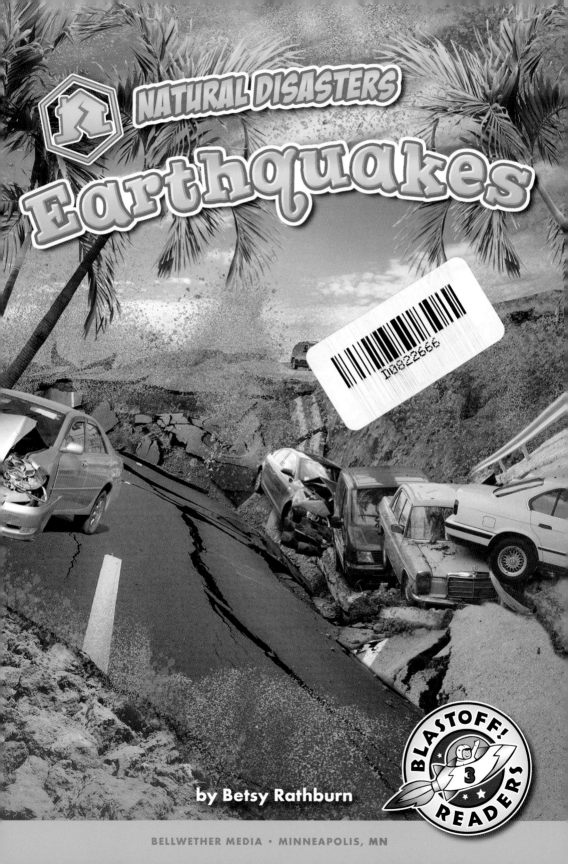

NATURAL DISASTERS

Earthquakes

by Betsy Rathburn

BELLWETHER MEDIA · MINNEAPOLIS, MN

Note to Librarians, Teachers, and Parents:

Blastoff! Readers are carefully developed by literacy experts and combine standards-based content with developmentally appropriate text.

Level 1 provides the most support through repetition of high-frequency words, light text, predictable sentence patterns, and strong visual support.

Level 2 offers early readers a bit more challenge through varied simple sentences, increased text load, and less repetition of high-frequency words.

Level 3 advances early-fluent readers toward fluency through increased text and concept load, less reliance on visuals, longer sentences, and more literary language.

Level 4 builds reading stamina by providing more text per page, increased use of punctuation, greater variation in sentence patterns, and increasingly challenging vocabulary.

Level 5 encourages children to move from "learning to read" to "reading to learn" by providing even more text, varied writing styles, and less familiar topics.

Whichever book is right for your reader, Blastoff! Readers are the perfect books to build confidence and encourage a love of reading that will last a lifetime!

This edition first published in 2020 by Bellwether Media, Inc.

No part of this publication may be reproduced in whole or in part without written permission of the publisher. For information regarding permission, write to Bellwether Media, Inc., Attention: Permissions Department, 6012 Blue Circle Drive, Minnetonka, MN 55343.

Library of Congress Cataloging-in-Publication Data

Names: Rathburn, Betsy, author.
Title: Earthquakes / by Betsy Rathburn.
Description: Minneapolis, MN : Bellwether Media, Inc., [2020] | Series:
  Blastoff! Readers: Natural Disasters | Audience: Ages 5-8. | Audience: K
  to grade 3. | Includes bibliographical references and index.
Identifiers: LCCN 2019001504 (print) | LCCN 2019008746 (ebook) | ISBN
  9781618915665 (ebook) | ISBN 9781644870259 (hardcover : alk. paper) | ISBN
  9781618917461 (pbk. : alk. paper)
Subjects: LCSH: Earthquakes--Juvenile literature. | Natural disasters--Juvenile literature.
Classification: LCC QE521.3 (ebook) | LCC QE521.3 .R375 2020 (print) | DDC
  551.22--dc23
LC record available at https://lccn.loc.gov/2019001504

Editor: Al Albertson   Designer: Josh Brink

Printed in the United States of America, North Mankato, MN.

Table of Contents

What Are Earthquakes?

Earthquakes are events that make the ground shake. They happen along **faults**. These cracks are all over Earth's surface.

Most earthquakes strike around the **Ring of Fire**.

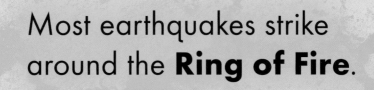

Ring of Fire

N
W   E
S

Ring of Fire = ☐

How Do Earthquakes Form?

tectonic plates

Earth has seven major **tectonic plates**. They move deep below Earth's surface. Sometimes the plates get stuck. Energy builds as they try to move.

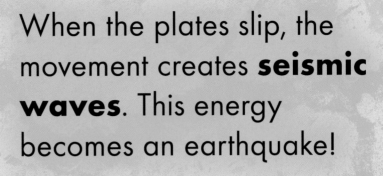

When the plates slip, the movement creates **seismic waves**. This energy becomes an earthquake!

recording seismic waves

Seismic waves travel outward from the earthquake's **focus**. They reach the **epicenter** on Earth's surface.

How Earthquakes Form

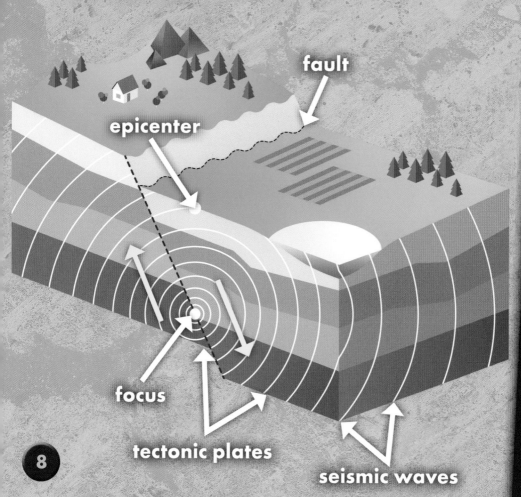

fault

epicenter

focus

tectonic plates

seismic waves

Most damage happens at the epicenter. But strong seismic waves are felt many miles away!

Earthquake Damage

fallen buildings

Earthquakes can cause a lot of damage. The shaking ground can make buildings fall down. People in old, weak buildings are in the most danger.

Aftershocks add more damage. Deep cracks may form in the ground. These can ruin roads and stop travel!

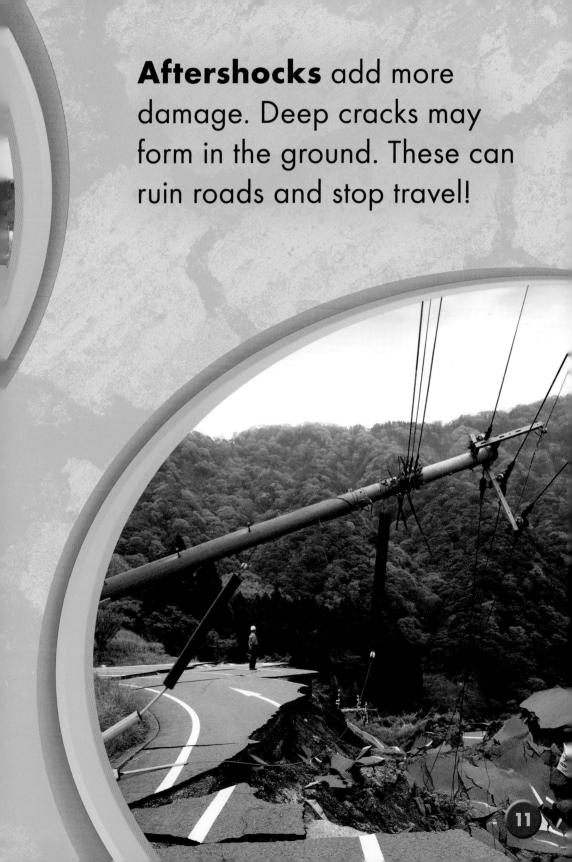

Some earthquakes bring flooding to coastal areas. Floods sweep houses, cars, and people away.

flood

landslide

Landslides and **avalanches** are also common after earthquakes. They cause falling rocks and snow in mountain areas. They can be deadly!

The **Richter Scale** helps describe earthquake strength. It rates an earthquake based on its **magnitude** recorded by **seismographs**.

Some earthquakes cannot be felt. Others completely destroy entire cities.

seismograph

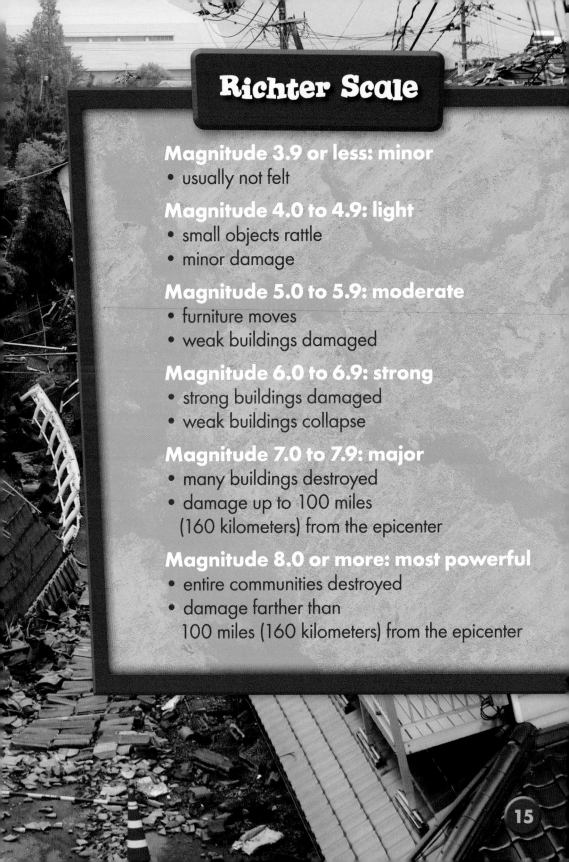

Richter Scale

Magnitude 3.9 or less: minor
- usually not felt

Magnitude 4.0 to 4.9: light
- small objects rattle
- minor damage

Magnitude 5.0 to 5.9: moderate
- furniture moves
- weak buildings damaged

Magnitude 6.0 to 6.9: strong
- strong buildings damaged
- weak buildings collapse

Magnitude 7.0 to 7.9: major
- many buildings destroyed
- damage up to 100 miles (160 kilometers) from the epicenter

Magnitude 8.0 or more: most powerful
- entire communities destroyed
- damage farther than 100 miles (160 kilometers) from the epicenter

Predicting Disaster

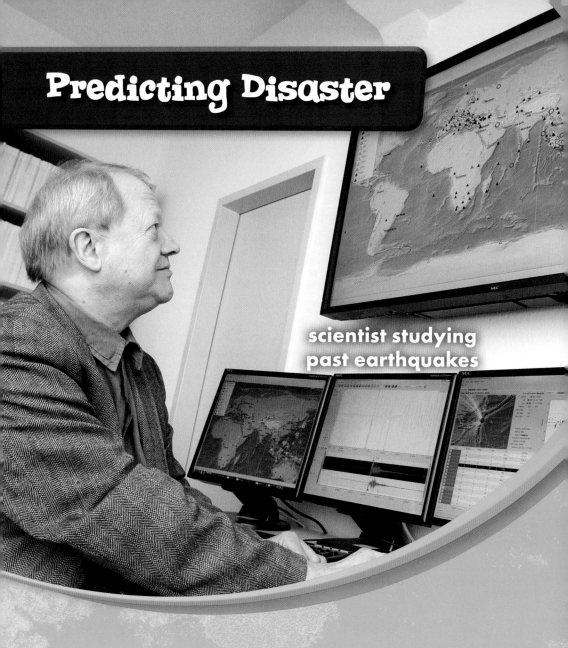

scientist studying
past earthquakes

Scientists cannot **predict** earthquakes. But they can warn people of other coming danger.

Scientists are on the lookout for floods and landslides. They can warn people to find safety!

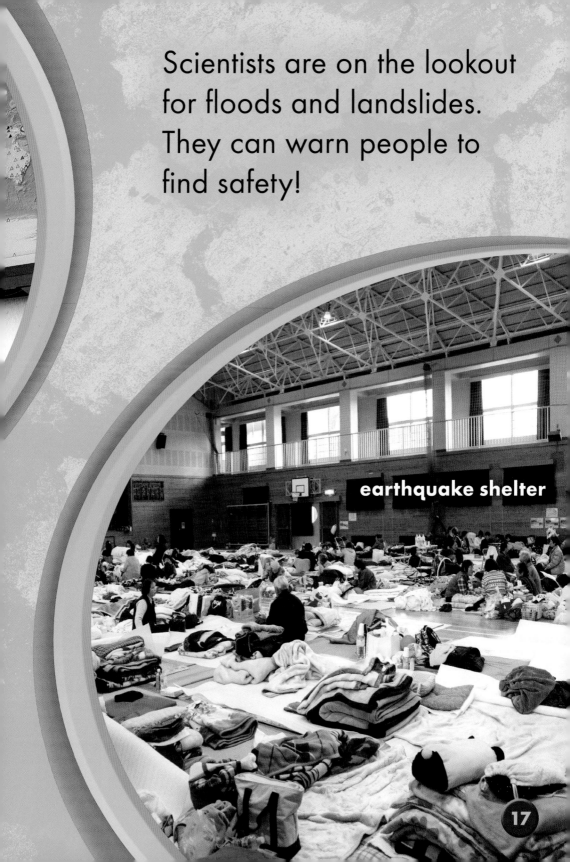

earthquake shelter

Earthquakes can be dangerous. But there are ways to stay safe.

Scientists keep detailed records of past earthquakes. Keeping records and making predictions helps to keep people safe!

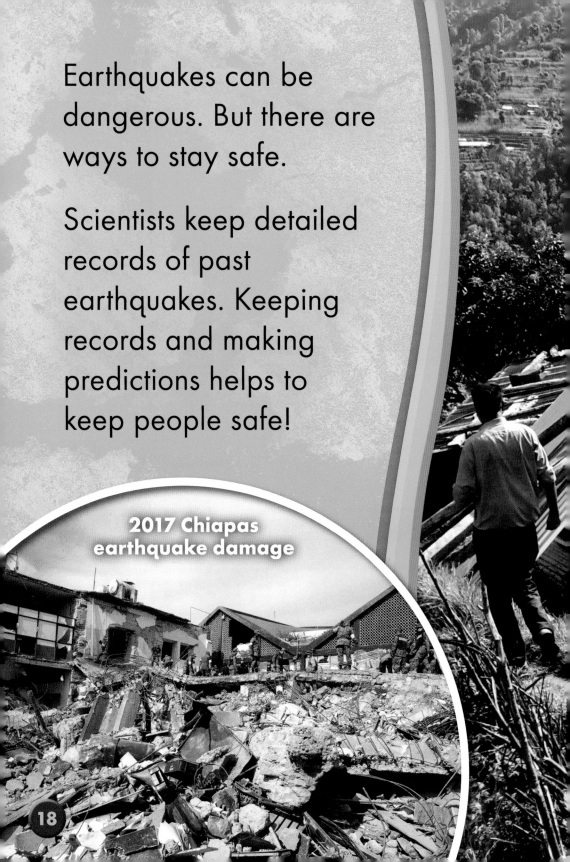

2017 Chiapas earthquake damage

Earthquake Profile

Name: 2017 Chiapas earthquake

Dates: September 8, 2017

Location: epicenter in the Gulf of Tehuantepec near Chiapas, Mexico

Magnitude: 8.2

Damage to Property:
- more than 40,000 homes destroyed
- thousands of schools damaged
- billions of dollars in damage

Damage to People:
- more than 300 lives lost
- thousands of students missed school
- lost jobs and homes lead to future problems

Objects often fall from high places during earthquakes. It is safest to hide under heavy furniture like tables.

Earthquake damage cannot be stopped. People must rebuild after disaster strikes!

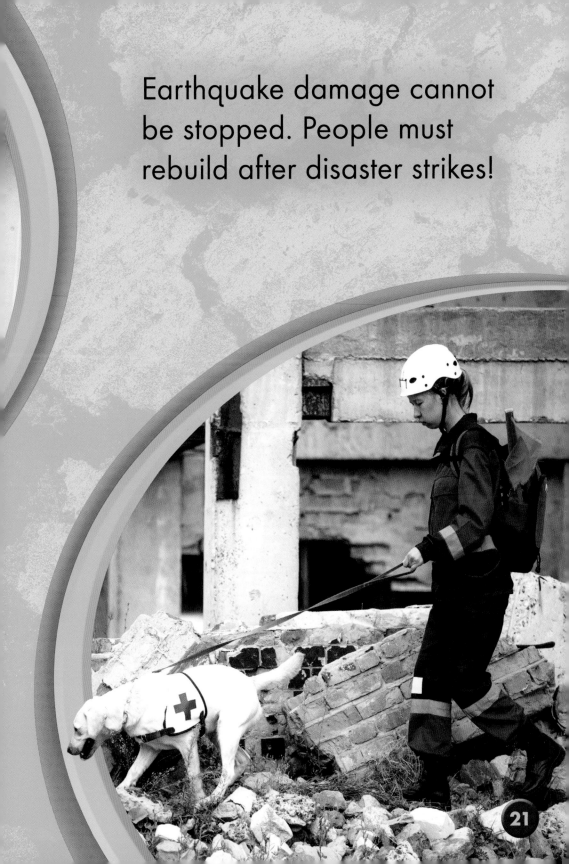

Glossary

aftershocks—smaller earthquakes that come after a large earthquake

avalanches—events in which ice, snow, and rocks suddenly fall down a mountain

epicenter—the place on Earth's surface right above where an earthquake begins

faults—the breaks in Earth's crust that separate tectonic plates

focus—the area below Earth's surface where an earthquake begins

landslides—events in which rocks, dirt, and mud suddenly fall down a mountain

magnitude—the power of an earthquake

predict—to use information to guess what may happen

Richter Scale—the scale that measures the magnitude of earthquakes

Ring of Fire—the area around the Pacific Ocean where most earthquakes occur; the Ring of Fire gets its name from the many volcanoes around its edges.

seismic waves—waves of energy in the ground or along Earth's surface caused by earthquakes

seismographs—tools used to measure the power of seismic waves

tectonic plates—the layers of Earth's crust that move

To Learn More

AT THE LIBRARY
Baker, John R. *The World's Worst Earthquakes.* Mankato, Minn.: Capstone Press, 2017.

Brooks, Susie. *Earthquakes and Volcanoes.* New York, N.Y.: PowerKids Press, 2016.

Perish, Patrick. *Survive an Earthquake.* Minneapolis, Minn.: Bellwether Media, 2017.

ON THE WEB

FACTSURFER

Factsurfer.com gives you a safe, fun way to find more information.

1. Go to www.factsurfer.com.

2. Enter "earthquakes" into the search box and click Q.

3. Select your book cover to see a list of related web sites.

Index

The images in this book are reproduced through the courtesy of: Fotos593, cover (background); riekephotos, cover (hero); Andrei Nekrassov, cover (dirt); Dutourdumonde Photography, CIP (background); Kaentian Street, CIP (dirt); Nigel Spiers/ Alamy, p. 4; dikobraziy, p. 5; ghost design, p. 6; EyeEm/ Alamy, p. 7; VectorMine, p. 8; Jake Lyell/ Alamy, p. 9; yankane, p. 10; austinding, pp. 11, 15; The Asahi Shimbun/ Getty Images, p. 12; Thomas Dekiere, p. 13; Achmad Ibrahim/ AP Images, p. 14; dpa picture alliance archive/ Alamy, p. 16; amata90, p. 17; presidenciamx/ Alamy, p. 18; Kristin F. Ruhs, p. 19; maroke, p. 20; home for heroes, p. 21.